A Crabtree Branches Book

Today's Stars

SELENA GOMEZ

Ellen Rodger

Crabtree Publishing
crabtreebooks.com

School-to-Home Support for Caregivers and Teachers

This high-interest book is designed to motivate striving students with engaging topics while building fluency, vocabulary, and an interest in reading. Here are a few questions and activities to help the reader build upon his or her comprehension skills.

Before Reading:

- *What do I think this book is about?*
- *What do I know about this topic?*
- *What do I want to learn about this topic?*
- *Why am I reading this book?*

During Reading:

- *I wonder why...*
- *I'm curious to know...*
- *How is this like something I already know?*
- *What have I learned so far?*

After Reading:

- *What was the author trying to teach me?*
- *What are some details?*
- *How did the photographs and captions help me understand more?*
- *Read the book again and look for the vocabulary words.*
- *What questions do I still have?*

Extension Activities:

- *What was your favorite part of the book? Write a paragraph on it.*
- *Draw a picture of your favorite thing you learned from the book.*

TABLE OF CONTENTS

LIKABLE LEADER

From child actor to billionaire, Selena Gomez has come a long way. Selena is an actor, singer, television **producer**, and businessperson. She's also a barrier buster and record breaker!

Selena busted barriers in becoming the most Emmy-nominated **Latina** television producer. She has repeatedly broken the record for the most-followed woman, actress, and singer on Instagram. She currently has more than 417 million followers!

Fortune *magazine declared Selena one of the world's youngest self-made billionaires at age 32.*

People like Selena because she is relatable, or able to show her true self. She has overcome many **obstacles** in her life. Selena has used her experiences to become a better person.

Fun Facts

Selena has broken 16 Guinness World Records. In 2016, she had the most likes for a female actor on Facebook at 61.4 million!

A STAR IS BORN

Selena Marie Gomez was born on July 22, 1992, in Grand Prairie, Texas. Her parents, Amanda Cornett and Ricardo Gomez, divorced when Selena was five. Selena lived with her mother in Texas until they later moved to California.

Selena lived in Grand Prairie until she was 13.

Fun Facts

Selena was named after Texan **Tejano** singer Selena Quintanilla-Pérez. Both have Mexican American roots.

Selena's early life was difficult. Her family did not have a lot of money. Her mother worked three jobs. But they had each other. Selena was close with her father and grandparents, who also cared for her and loved her.

After noticing Selena's interest in performing when she was around six, Selena's mom encouraged her to pursue acting.

When Selena was 10, she was hired to act on the children's TV show *Barney & Friends*. She then moved on to small roles in films and on several Disney series.

Barney & Friends *featured Selena (second from right) with fellow child star Demi Lovato (center).*

At 15, Selena earned a starring role on the Disney television series *Wizards of Waverly Place*. At the same time, she did voice acting for animated shows and launched a music career.

Selena voiced the character of Mavis Dracula in the Hotel Transylvania *movies.*

Wizards of Waverly Place ran for four seasons. Selena learned to act on the show, but it wasn't her only entertainment **venture**.

Wizards of Waverly Place *earned an Emmy Award for Outstanding Children's Program two years in a row.*

At 16, Selena formed a band called Selena Gomez & the Scene. The band won the Favorite Breakout Artist award at the 2010 People's Choice Awards. Selena quickly learned how to balance her music and acting careers.

Selena Gomez & the Scene released their first album, Kiss and Tell, *in September 2009.*

Selena and her half-sister Gracie Elliot Teefey

Fun Facts

Both of Selena's parents remarried and she has two younger half-sisters and a stepbrother.

OVERCOMING OBSTACLES

In 2013, Selena released her first single from her debut solo album *Stars Dance*. "Come & Get It" quickly reached top ten on the charts. She then launched a tour.

The Stars Dance Tour was cut short when, at 21, Selena was diagnosed with lupus. This is a disease that occurs when the body's immune system attacks its own tissues and organs. Selena also struggled with her mental health.

May is Lupus Awareness Month. People are encouraged to wear purple to make others aware of the disease.

Despite her health challenges, when she felt well, Selena moved forward with her career. She released two more solo albums between 2015 and 2020. She also launched another concert tour in 2016.

Selena was named Woman of the Year in 2017 by the music magazine Billboard.

In 2017, Selena received a kidney **transplant**. Her kidney had been damaged by lupus. As she recovered, Selena focused on acting work and producing movies and TV shows.

Selena's kidney donor was her friend Francia Raisa.

AWARD WINNER

Selena has been nominated for and won many awards for her music, acting, and producing. Early in her career, she won 18 Teen Choice Awards and holds the record (12) for Kids' Choice Awards.

As an adult, Selena started being recognized for her producing and **philanthropy** work. TV shows she produced began receiving Emmy nominations.

Selena has received five Emmy nominations over the course of her career. An Emmy is an award for outstanding achievement for television in the United States.

In 2020, Selena started a makeup company called Rare Beauty. Other businesses she was involved in were successful as well. In 2024, Selena joined the very small group of musicians who are billionaires, including Rihanna, Taylor Swift, Jay-Z, and Bruce Springsteen.

Selena named Rare Beauty after her third album, Rare.

Fun Facts

Rare Beauty has won many beauty industry awards for makeup. *TIME* magazine named it one of the most influential companies of 2024.

GIVING BACK

With great wealth, Selena feels great responsibility. She began helping others early in her career. Selena served as an **ambassador** for UNICEF. She traveled to countries such as Ghana, Chile, and Nepal to support children's rights, health, and education.

Selena first became a UNICEF ambassador in 2009.

Selena is passionate about her charity work. Some of the causes she has promoted include groups that fight against **genocide** and environmental harm.

By sharing her private experiences with her mental and physical health, Selena has fought **stigma**. This has helped others who share her struggle not to feel shame.

Both Selena and her mom have spoken publicly about Selena's mental health struggles.

Selena established the Rare Impact Fund. It helps schools, communities, and suicide prevention groups. Through the fund, she has pledged $100 million to services that provide mental health support to young people.

One percent of all Rare Beauty sales are donated to the Rare Impact Fund.

Selena has said that her biggest dream is to "make a positive impact in the world." She does this through her music, acting, and by helping others.

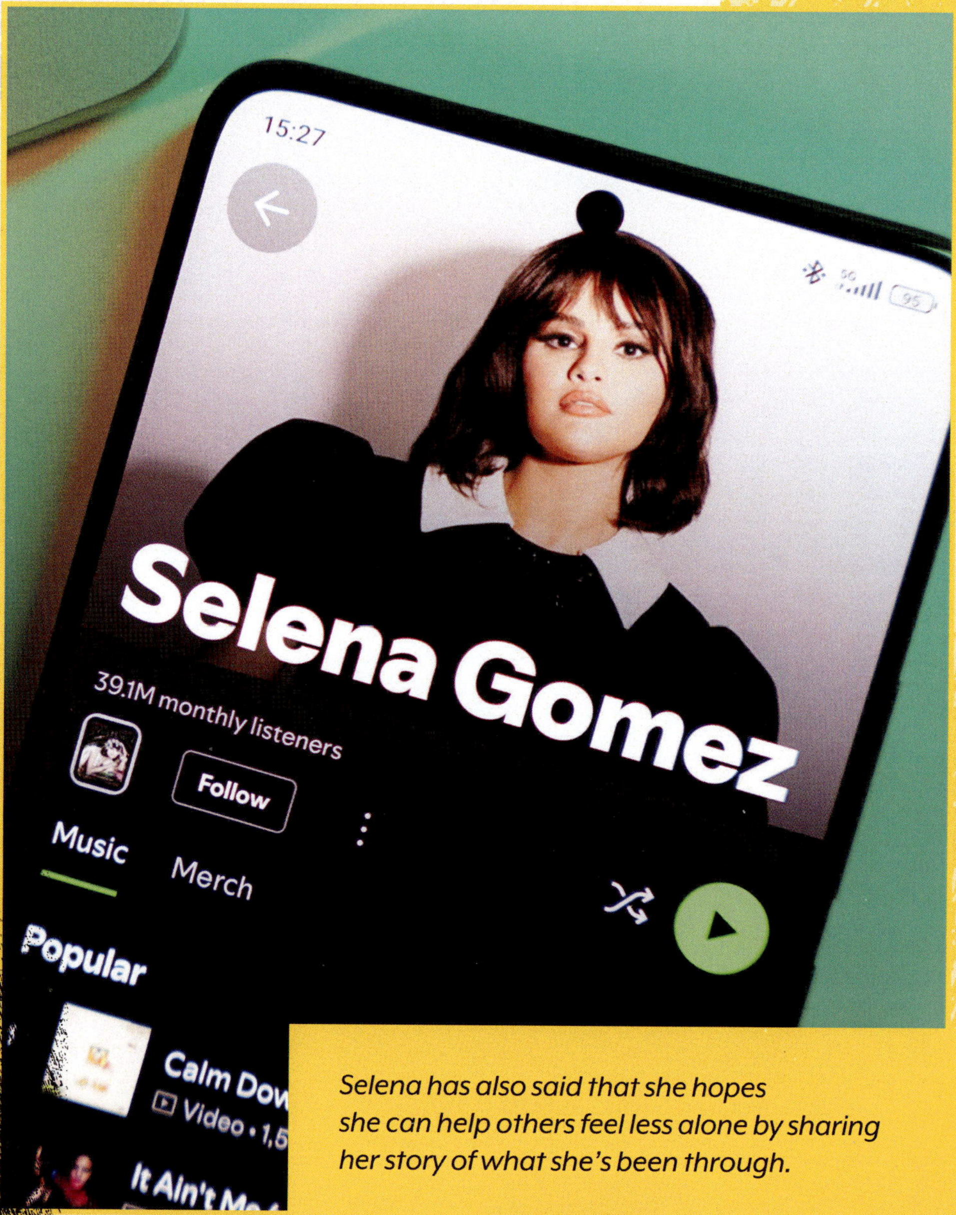

Selena has also said that she hopes she can help others feel less alone by sharing her story of what she's been through.

Fun Facts

Selena made a documentary film about her mental health, called *My Mind & Me*. She has also launched a website called Wondermind to help people work on their mental health.

GLOSSARY

ambassador (am-BAS-uh-der): A person who is chosen to represent or promote a specified activity

genocide (JEN-uh-sahyd): Violent crimes committed against people who belong to a particular racial, political, or cultural group, with the intent to destroy the existence of the group

influential (in-floo-EN-shall): Having the power to impact the actions, behavior, or opinions of others

Latina (la-TEE-nuh): Relating to females of Latin American descent or origin, especially those from the United States

obstacle (OB-stuh-kuhl): Something that makes it difficult to do or achieve something

philanthropy (fi-LAN-thruh-pee): Giving or donating money or time to something that helps others

producer (pruh-DOO-ser): A person who oversees the making of a movie or television show

stigma (STIG-muh): Negative attitudes or beliefs about a person or group of people because of their situation in life

Tejano (tey-HAH-noh): A form of popular music featuring accordions that originated in Mexico

transplant (TRANS-plant): A medical operation where an organ is removed from one person's body and put in the body of another

venture (VEN-cher): A new project that involves some risk

INDEX

WEBSITES TO VISIT

https://www.biography.com/musicians/selena-gomez

https://www.thefactsite.com/selena-gomez-facts/

https://rareimpactfund.org

ABOUT THE AUTHOR

Ellen Rodger won a bank-sponsored short story contest at age nine. It was the last thing her bank ever gave her for free, but it kicked-started a career in newspaper, magazine, and book publishing. Ellen has written hundreds of books for curious young people, on topics as varied as the history of the potato, urban wildlife, refugees, the Great Lakes, and explorers.

Crabtree Publishing

crabtreebooks.com 800-387-7650

Written by: Ellen Rodger
Designed by: Kathy Walsh
Series Development: James Earley
Editor: Melissa Boyce
Educational Consultant: Marie Lemke M.Ed.
Production manager: Candice Campbell

Hardcover: 978-1-0398-8033-7
Paperback: 978-1-0398-8393-2
Ebook (pdf): 978-1-0398-8153-2
Epub: 978-1-0398-8273-7

Printed in the U.S.A./CP2025

Published in Canada
Crabtree Publishing
616 Welland Ave.
St. Catharines, Ontario
L2M 5V6

Published in the United States
Crabtree Publishing
347 Fifth Ave
Suite 1402-145
New York, NY 10016

Library and Archives Canada Cataloguing in Publication
Available at Library and Archives Canada

Library of Congress Cataloging-in-Publication Data
Available at the Library of Congress

Photographs
Alamy: Everett Collection Inc p 11, Newscom p 12, JOHN ANGELILLO p 16, ZUMA p 26, Barry King 27, AFF p 29
Shutterstock: DFree, cover, title page, p 13 (bottom), p 19; Kathy Hutchins, TOC, p 18, p 20, p 31; Joe Seer, p 4, p 21 (right); Featureflash Photo Agency, p 5, p 15, p 22; John Steel, P 6; Tinseltown, p 7, p 12; Lisa T Snow, p 9 (top) s_bukley, p 10, p 14, p 24; Jaguar PS, p 21 (left); Frylodi, p 23; Rokas Tenys, p 28
All other images from Shutterstock